Karina Garcia's

MUST-TRY DIYs

SIZZLE PRESS

For my loving and supportive viewers. You inspire me every day. I hope this book inspires you! —K.G.

SIZZLE PRESS

An imprint of Bonnier Publishing USA
251 Park Avenue South, New York, NY 10010
Copyright © 2017 by Karina Garcia
Text by Aubre Andrus
All rights reserved, including the right of reproduction in whole or in part in any form.
SIZZLE PRESS is a trademark of Bonnier Publishing USA, and associated colophon is a trademark of Bonnier Publishing USA.
Play-Doh is a registered trademark of HASBRO, INC.
M&M'S is a registered trademark of Mars, Incorporated.
emoji is a registered trademark of the emoji company GmbH.
Jolly Rancher is a registered trademark of The Hershey Company.
HERSHEY'S is a registered trademark of The Hershey Company.
TWIX is a registered trademark of Mars, Incorporated.
SNICKERS is a registered trademark of Mars, Incorporated.
Kit Kat is a registered trademark of Nestlé.
Elmer's Glue-All is a registered trademark of Elmer's Products, Inc.
VELCRO® and VELCRO® design are registered trademarks of Velcro BVBA.
CRAFT CITY is a registered trademark of Brandable, Inc.
Manufactured in the United States of America VEP 0917
First Edition
10 9 8 7 6 5 4 3 2 1
ISBN 978-1-4998-0700-4
sizzlepressbooks.com
bonnierpublishingusa.com

KARINA GARCIA'S
MUST-TRY
DIYS

HEY, GIRL, HEY!

You guys already know I love making slime, but I also love making all kinds of DIY projects. This book is filled with my favorite crafts, plus a ton of new stuff! Honestly, you guys inspire me every day, so use these projects to get your creative juices flowing.

PROJECT KEY

Cost:

$ Means the project is almost free—you can probably find this stuff at home if you're crafty like me!

$$ Means you might need to buy a few inexpensive items.

$$$ Means you'll have to head to the store to pick up some special ingredients.

Ease:

easy   Means the project is pretty easy.

medium   Means you'll need a little bit of skill or practice.

hard   Means the project is more challenging.

Time:

I've included a timetable about how long each project takes. It's always best to have extra time. Some crafts have to dry overnight.

HERE ARE SOME TIPS BEFORE YOU DIVE IN

1. Be sure to read all of the instructions before you begin a project. That way you can make sure you have all the supplies you need, and you'll be less likely to make mistakes.

2. Make sure you have enough time. Your crafts will turn out better if you don't feel rushed.

3. Be creative! Feel free to put your own spin on anything.

4. Use and share your projects. There are tons of tips and guides throughout the book to help with this. Be proud of the things you make!

AND HERE ARE THE BIG THINGS

Don't forget to ask your parents for permission before you start making any of these DIYs! I don't want you to get into any trouble. ;-)

Always be safe! All steps using the following tools or ingredients should be done by an adult: superglue, hot glue and hot glue gun, hobby knife, scissors, oven, microwave, and spray paint. No getting hurt, ok?

Now let's go make a mess!

<3,
Karina

TABLE OF CONTENTS

MEET KARINA!

I live in Riverside, California, with my parents and siblings, and I have a DIY YouTube channel called TheKarinaBear.

I've been crafting for about two years. It all started with beauty DIYs, and within months I became interested in slime. There weren't a lot of slime tutorials or recipes online when I began, so I followed a really basic recipe and then started throwing random stuff in it to create different textures.

I uploaded my first video to YouTube on February 11, 2015 and my first slime video on August 12, 2015. Since then, I've uploaded hundreds of videos and built a following. My followers drive me and inspire me every day!

Nowadays crafting is my career. I travel all over the country going to events and meeting my fans. I even wrote a slime recipe book!

My twin sister, Mayra, also has a YouTube channel, mayratouchofglam. Her beauty videos are awesome. She was the one who first encouraged me to start making videos of my own!

This is my litter sister, Jasmin. Whenever she has friends come over, I'm like, "Hey, I have so much slime. Do you guys want some?" They always end up leaving with slime.

My boyfriend, Raul, is my best friend and the best business partner ever. He helps film all of my videos and has grown to love crafting himself. He is an amazing person who literally cleans up my messy craft/filming room because I'm honestly so messy. He's my right hand.

I've been making crafts since before I started a YouTube channel. I made my own makeup, makeup organizers, and vanity. One day I made lipsticks so bomb, I posted a tutorial. I challenge myself to make new crafts every day. Sometimes they're simple. Sometimes they're more complicated. I just love the process of getting my hands dirty and figuring out how to make my ideas a reality.

I make everything at home—you can, too! Making DIYs taught me to follow my passion, and it's changed my life. I really encourage you to do the same. I hope this book helps!

HAIR, FACE, AND ACCESSORIES

SLIME BRACELETS

If you can't get enough of my slime tutorials, you'll love this DIY.
These bracelets make for great gifts for your friends, too!

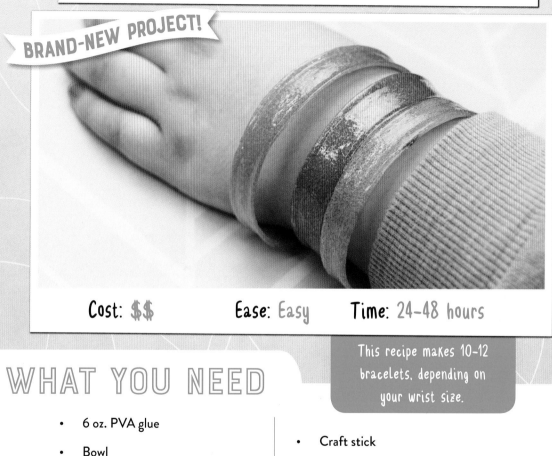

BRAND-NEW PROJECT!

Cost: $$ **Ease**: Easy   **Time**: 24-48 hours

This recipe makes 10-12 bracelets, depending on your wrist size.

WHAT YOU NEED

- 6 oz. PVA glue
- Bowl
- ½ tsp. baking soda
- 3 tbsp. contact lens solution
- Liquid food coloring

- Craft stick
- Elastic cord or string
- Rubber kitchen gloves (optional)
- Scissors

HERE'S HOW TO MAKE IT!

1 Pour glue and baking soda into a bowl. Mix until baking soda dissolves.

2 Squirt in contact lens solution and slowly stir, adding a little bit at a time until the slime begins forming. Once the slime starts to come together, it will look like a blob and you can to knead it with your hands.

You will know it's fully slime when it doesn't stick to your hands anymore!

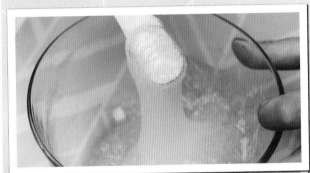

3 Separate the slime on the table into small pieces, one for each bracelet. Then add 3 drops of a food coloring of your choice to each piece. Fold in the food coloring with your hands.

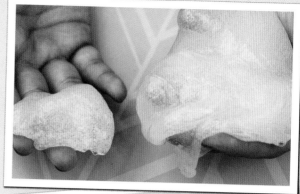

Protect the surface you are working on to make sure the food coloring doesn't stain. You can wear rubber kitchen gloves to protect your hands.

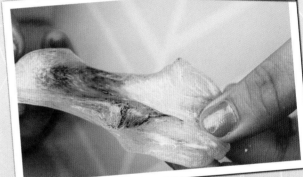

4 Roll the small pieces of slime into long tubes. Make the bracelets a little longer than what you think you'll need. Let them sit for a day or two to harden.

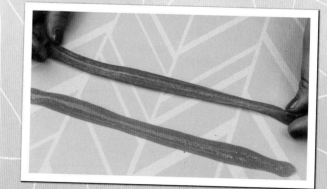

5 Once each bracelet has hardened, fold over one end of the bracelet slightly. Snip the middle of this folded piece with scissors, then unfold the bracelet. There should now be a small hole. Repeat on the other side.

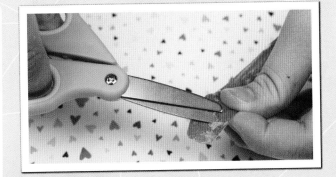

6 String the elastic cord or string through the holes on each end of every bracelet. Tie each one into a double knot and trim any excess.

That's it! So easy and so cute!

DIY FACE PAINT

This is a super-easy and affordable project.
Who's ready for the game this weekend?*

BRAND-NEW PROJECT!

Cost: $ Ease: Easy   Time: 24 hours

WHAT YOU NEED

This recipe makes enough for about 10 different colors.

- 3 tbsp. cornstarch
- 3 tbsp. face lotion
- ½ tsp. vegetable oil
- Craft stick

- Medium-sized bowl
- 10 one-oz. plastic containers with lids
- Liquid food coloring
- Paintbrush

*Once you've made the paint, you should test it on your arm and wait a day before using it on your face.

HERE'S HOW TO MAKE IT!

1 In the bowl, mix equal parts cornstarch and face lotion until it becomes thick.

2 Now stir in the vegetable oil. This will keep the face paint from cracking. You're now done with the base!

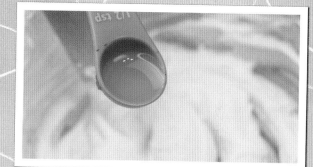

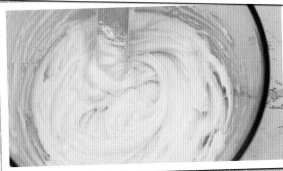

3 Split the base evenly into mini plastic containers, one container for every color you want. Add no more than 3 drops of food coloring total to each container and stir with the craft stick.

You only need a tiny bit of food coloring—it goes a long way! If you put in too much, you can stain your face.

4 Time to test! To make sure the paint doesn't hurt your skin, put a tiny bit on your wrist. If it itches or burns, wash it off immediately and tell an adult. Otherwise, wait 24 hours and check your skin. If you have no reaction, you can use your paint!

Make sure to put the lids on your paints so they don't dry out overnight.

5 Apply it to your face with a paintbrush. Make sure to keep the paint out of your eyes.

Wow, what an easy and affordable project!

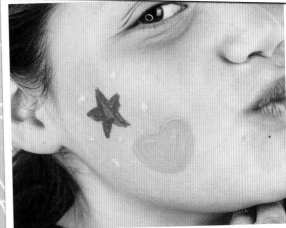

HAIR CHALK

Get the (temporary) hair color of your
dreams in just five minutes!

BRAND-NEW PROJECT!

Cost: $ Ease: Easy Time: 5 min.

WHAT YOU NEED

- Colored sidewalk chalk
- Butter knife
- Bowl

- Spray bottle filled with water
- Hair spray
- Small paintbrush or makeup brush (optional)

HERE'S HOW TO MAKE IT!

1 Using the chalk color of your choice, take the butter knife and scrape it against the chalk over the bowl so small chalk particles begin collecting in the bowl.

2 Now make sure your hair is damp. I like to use a spray bottle filled with water to spritz hair.

3 It's time to add the chalk powder! Using a wet paintbrush, makeup brush, or your fingers, reach into the bowl and add the powder to your hair. Since your hair is damp, the powder will attach to your hair easily.

If you're having a hard time getting the color to stay, try massaging the powder into hair with your fingers!

4 Wow, look at those pretty colors! Lock in the chalk with some hair spray. And that's it!

Such a fun look.

8

Almost done! Glue on the buttons to the circle paper cutouts with PVA glue. Use clear glue if you don't want it to show. Let dry. Now you won't poke your fingers as you spin!

Play with it. Erase with it. This fidget spinner is so useful!

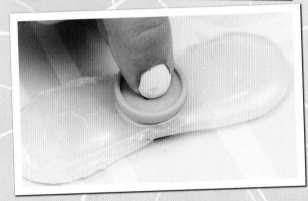

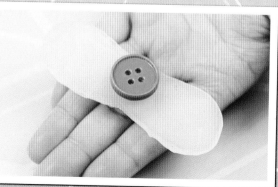

SUPER-SIMPLE FIDGET SPINNER

You guys are going to love this one—a super-easy
and inexpensive fidget spinner!*

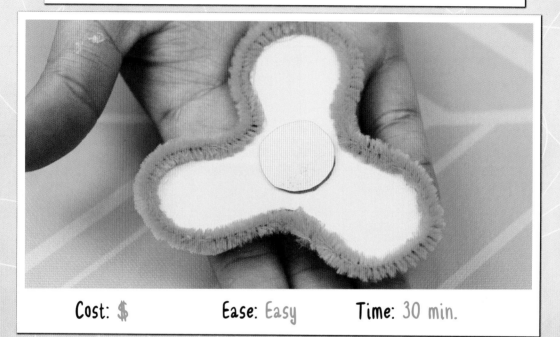

Cost: $ Ease: Easy   Time: 30 min.

WHAT YOU NEED

- Fidget Spinner template (directions on page 108)
- Penny
- Construction paper

- Scissors
- Toothpick
- Plastic coffee stirrer
- Pen

- PVA glue
- Chenille stem (optional)
- Superglue (optional)

You'll need an adult to help you with this project.

HERE'S HOW TO MAKE IT!

1

Use the fidget spinner template as the base of this spinner! Pierce the center of the fidget spinner with a toothpick. Remove toothpick from the fidget spinner and insert the coffee stirrer. You want the fidget spinner to be loose on the stirrer so that it spins easily.

If this is your last fidget spinner stencil on page 109, make an extra for future projets.

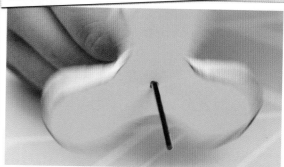

Trace a penny onto construction paper 4 times. Cut out the circles and pierce each one carefully in the center with a pen.

Make sure the construction paper is lying on a flat surface and not in your own hand!

Slide paper circles onto either side of the coffee stirrer, but make sure to leave a tiny amount of space so the spinner can still spin. Keep the paper in place by dabbing a small dot of PVA glue at the center of the paper and onto the coffee stirrer. Let dry.

4 Now cut off the excess coffee stirrer with scissors. Cut as close to the paper as possible.

5 Almost done! Glue the remaining 2 paper circles to the existing paper circles. Let dry. Now you won't poke your fingers as you spin.

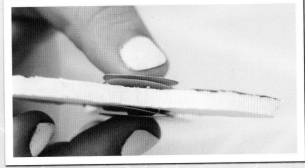

6 **ASK AN ADULT FOR HELP HERE.**

Optional! Do the edges of your fidget spinner look rough? Wrap a chenille stem around the edges and fix in place with superglue. Adorable!

And so simple!

SODA POP FIDGET SPINNER

Start saving your pop tops so you can spin your life away
with this super-affordable DIY fidget spinner!*

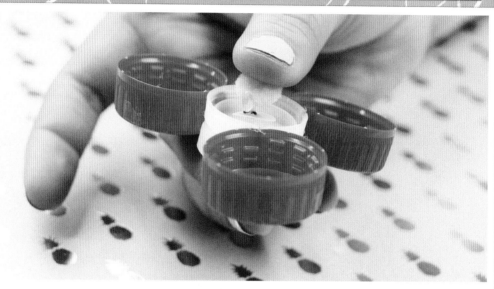

Cost: $ Ease: Medium   Time: 20 min.

WHAT YOU NEED

- Construction paper
- Scissors
- 3 soda bottle caps
- 2 water bottle caps

- Thick needle
- Plastic coffee stirrer
- Toothpick
- Hot glue and hot glue gun

- Superglue
- 2 mini pom-poms
- 3 pennies or small matching coins

*You'll need an adult to help you with this project.

1

Using a water bottle top as a stencil, trace 2 circles onto construction paper. Cut out the circles slightly smaller than the stencil. Pierce each one carefully in the center with a pen.

Make sure the construction paper is laying on a flat surface and not in your own hand when cutting.

2 **ASK AN ADULT FOR HELP HERE.**

Carefully pierce the center of both water bottle caps with a thick needle.

Make sure bottle caps are laying on a flat surface and not in your own hand.

3 Insert the toothpick, then wiggle it around to make the holes larger. You'll know it's ready when each cap spins freely.

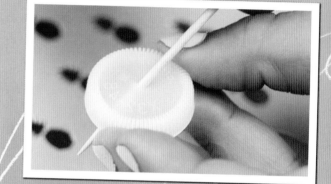

4 **ASK AN ADULT FOR HELP HERE.**

Next, string the water bottle caps onto the coffee stirrer with the flat surfaces facing each other. Using a hot glue gun, attach the flat surfaces together. Be sure not to cover the holes. Let it dry.

5

Slide paper circles onto either side of the coffee stirrer, but make sure to leave a tiny amount of space so the spinner can still spin. Keep the paper in place by dabbing a small dot of superglue at the center of the paper and onto the coffee stirrer. Let dry.

6

Now cut off the excess stirrer with scissors. Cut as close to the caps as possible.

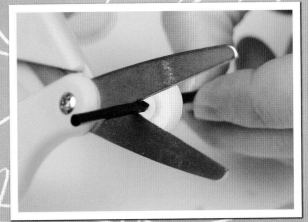

7 **ASK AN ADULT FOR HELP HERE.**

It's time to add some pom-poms! With superglue, attach a pom-pom on each side directly on the tip of the stirrer to prevent it from poking you.

8

On the water bottle caps, mark where to attach the 3 soda caps. They should be an even distance from each other.

Feel free to use the fidget spinner stencil on page 109 as a guide. And make sure the caps are all facing up or down—you want them all to face the same direction!

9
ASK AN ADULT FOR HELP HERE.

Using a hot glue gun, attach the edges of the soda caps to the edges of the water bottle caps. Let it dry.

Now it looks like a fidget spinner, but it doesn't spin like one! That means it's time to add some weight.

10
ASK AN ADULT FOR HELP HERE.

Using superglue, attach a penny to the inside of each soda cap. Give it a spin. Much better, right?

I can't stop playing with this.

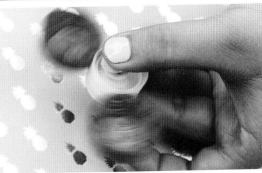

CHOCOLATE FIDGET SPINNER TREAT

Sit back and enjoy this delicious, edible treat after an exhausting day of spinning!
It won't spin like a toy, but it's even sweeter!*

BRAND-NEW PROJECT!

Cost: $$$ Ease: Medium   Time: 1 hour

WHAT YOU NEED

- Fidget Spinner template (directions on page 108)

- 1 chocolate bar

- M&M'S® or other small candy

- Microwave

- Microwave-safe bowl

- Nontoxic silicone putty (sold at craft stores and online)

- Oven mitt

You'll need an adult to help you with this project.

HERE'S HOW TO MAKE IT!

1 Wash your hands and work surface well. You'll be eating this craft.

2 Roll putty into a ball, then flatten it with your palm. Press the spinner template onto the putty firmly to create a mold. Let it cure for 20 minutes before beginning the next step.

The template should be level with the putty. Don't push it down too far!

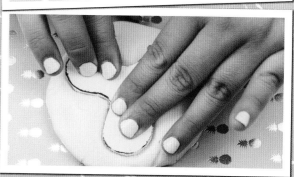

HERE'S HOW TO MAKE IT!

1 **ASK AN ADULT FOR HELP HERE.**

Using a hot glue gun, attach a small binder clip to the top center of the back of your phone case. Let it dry.

Make sure you're gluing the binder clip onto a phone case, and not directly onto your phone itself!

2 Add a piece of mini notebook paper to the clip—that's it!

Easiest and most convenient DIY ever!

CHALKBOARD PILLOW

This is such a cute way to make a throw pillow—
a throw pillow you can doodle on. How fun!*

BRAND-NEW PROJECT!

Cost: $$$ **Ease:** Medium   **Time:** 25 min.

WHAT YOU NEED

- 1 yard vinyl sheet (sold at fabric stores and online)
- Marker
- Ruler
- Scissors
- Hot glue and hot glue gun

- An old piece of clothing (such as a sweater or top) or cotton batting
- Chalkboard spray paint
- Sheets of newspaper
- Chalk

*You'll need an adult to help you with this project.

HERE'S HOW TO MAKE IT!

1 **ASK AN ADULT FOR HELP HERE.**

Using your ruler and marker, trace two 12" x 12" squares on the vinyl sheet. Cut them out.

Make sure the vinyl is lying on a flat surface and not in your own hand!

2 **ASK AN ADULT FOR HELP HERE.**

Place the two vinyl squares on top of each other. With a hot glue gun, glue three sides shut. Leave one side open. Let it dry for 15 minutes.

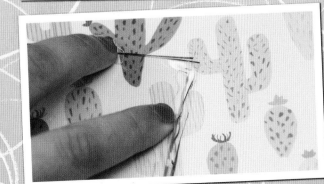

3

Turn the square inside out to conceal the edges of the vinyl sheet. Stuff the pillow with an old piece of clothing that you don't wear anymore. You can use cotton batting instead.

The clothing might get ruined, so make sure to get a parent's permission.

4

ASK AN ADULT FOR HELP HERE.

Glue the last edge shut with the hot glue gun. Fold the edge to make a smooth seam.

5

ASK AN ADULT FOR HELP HERE.

Go outside and cover your work surface with newspaper. Spray paint both sides of the pillow, one at a time. Let the first side dry before spraying the second side.

6

Now use it like you would use any chalkboard!

Write reminders to yourself or cute messages. This will liven up your room.

CLINGY NOTEBOOKS

This makes for a great way to organize! The VELCRO® keeps your notebooks stuck together in your backpack, and can help keep your subjects more organized. This is a super-easy life hack!

BRAND-NEW PROJECT!

Cost: $$ Ease: Easy   Time: 5 min.

WHAT YOU NEED

- 4 or more VELCRO® Sticky Back fasteners

- 3 notebooks

1 Attach the fuzzy part of the VELCRO® sticker to the back of the first notebook. I like to space them out by putting one between every two punch holes.

2 Attach the scratchy part of the VELCRO® sticker to the front of the second notebook. Make sure they correspond to the spacing of the first notebook. That's it!

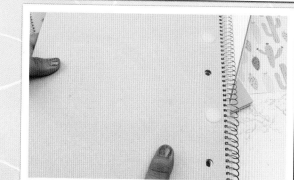

3 Repeat these steps to make as many notebooks as you want! So neat!

BEHIND THE SCENES

I love making school supplies. They're just so fun.

This tiny desk where I do all of my projects is where I made the Smiley Face Erasers.

This craft was seriously so easy, and I love the way they turned out. If it takes you a couple of tries to get it right, don't worry! Shaping clay takes practice and you'll get better at it!

DIY PRO TIPS

Ready to come up with your own DIYs? Yes! I encourage everyone to create projects and share them. Seriously, doing that has changed my life. Don't worry about people not liking your ideas— just do what you like!

It's okay if you weren't born with super-crazy creativity. You can still be crafty. If you're new to crafting, books and blogs about it are great places to start. It's way easier than you think when you're being walked through it.

I've been kind of creative my whole life, but I started these DIYs by re-creating other people's projects. So begin there, then try some of your own. Once you start getting into it, your creative juices will just start flowing and everything will come together. You just need some inspiration!

HERE'S HOW TO CREATE DIYS

DO WHAT YOU LOVE

Find what you're passionate about. For me, it all started with slime and then blossomed out from there!

TURN THIS INTO THAT

Whenever you see something cute that you like, think of a way you can transform it into something else. I'm always picking up things I like and thinking, "Okay, what can I do with this?" Usually I'm thinking about the craziest thing I could do with it. I'm constantly brainstorming and getting inspiration.

WRITE IT DOWN

I save my ideas on my phone. Otherwise I'll completely forget about them. Trust me, you think you'll remember them, but you won't!

START RIGHT AWAY

Whenever you think of something really cool and unique, get on it. You'll be excited about the idea, and the project will be more fun. Plus, only you have the ability to make your ideas a reality!

GIVE CREDIT

If you get inspired by someone else or are replicating their idea, you should always give credit to that person. Otherwise it's unfair to the person who created it.

DO NOT GIVE UP!

I often make the same mistake of thinking in my head that everything makes sense and it'll work out fine, but then once I end up trying it, it doesn't work out. Sometimes I feel like I have an amazing idea and then it goes so badly or nobody likes it. You just never know, honestly.

One time, I tried to make a rubber phone case. I invested hours in it, and it didn't work out. I do that all the time. I also tried to make a gummy phone case another time and that was a hot mess. A lot of the edible projects fail.

When things fail on me, a lot of times it stresses me out. I've had moments when something goes wrong and I will literally cry because it took me hours. Or I'll do something that looks like it's coming together and then in the end, it completely falls apart. And every single time, I'm like, "OMG, what am I doing wrong?!"

In that moment afterward—like for the first 10 minutes—I'll be mad. But after that happens, I'll just move on even though it's upsetting. I'll get over it eventually. It doesn't affect how I think about my crafting overall. I realize, "It's fine. Whatever. I'll try something new!"

Make sure to check out the Guides and Templates section. There are more tips there to help you out. I can't wait to see what you make!

GUIDES AND TEMPLATES

TOP 5 CRAFTING TOOLS

This is my must-have supply list. I use them in almost all my crafts. They're seriously so useful! As long as you have these 5 things, you can make something cute.

1. PAINT

I like acrylic paint. It's inexpensive and there are so many colors available. You'll also need some paintbrushes or sponges, which can be found in really big packs.

2. GLUE

Craft City is my favorite because there's so much you can do with it. That's my go-to glue—you can make any craft with it.

3. CRAFT STICKS

This sounds random but you can do so much with craft sticks! Stir things, paint things, build things—literally anything.

4. GLITTER

I'm always buying glitter. Glitter makes any craft look good. It's my fave. I love all kinds.

5. SCRAPBOOK PAPER

This is definitely a must! Not only can you make crafts with it, but you can also use it as a pretty background in photos or videos.

DIY STYLING TIPS

Want to share your crafts on Instagram or YouTube? Styling is all about making something look pretty for a photo or video. I do a lot of styling every day when I make my YouTube videos and when I work on projects like this book.

1. ALWAYS ADD SOME KIND OF COLORFUL BACKGROUND.

Plain white backgrounds wash out everything and look boring. Colorful backgrounds look high quality and make the lighting look better, too. The pop of color in the background makes a huge difference! Try posters, tablecloths, or scrapbook paper.

2. LIGHTING IS A GOOD THING.

I've heard that natural lighting is the best lighting, but I'm usually working at night. So I use softboxes, which are lights on a tripod. When you have really good lighting and a cute setup, even an iPhone can take a good picture!

3. ADD SOME PROPS.

I always try to make the focus of the photo look even prettier. After adding a colorful background, I'll add some accent pieces, too. If I'm taking a photo of a notebook, maybe I'll add a pencil and an apple to give the photo a school vibe. It looks so much cuter and more aesthetically pleasing.

SETTING UP A CRAFTING SPACE

It's so important to have a good area to make your crafts. That way you don't end up staining a carpet or scratching a desk! It's not hard to set up a space. Just follow these steps, and make sure to ask your parents before you use something for crafting.

1 FIND A GOOD SPOT.

All you need is a small table or desk. Make sure the surface is covered so you don't damage it while you're crafting.

2 GATHER SUPPLIES.

You don't need many! I shared my essential supplies on page 102. Those could all easily fit into a small storage bin. Always make sure to ask your parents if it's okay to use something for crafting.

3

GET MESSY.

Being creative is a messy process and that's okay. Just be sure to clean up when you're done. Try to contain the mess just to your crafting space. That will make cleaning a lot easier!

4

HAVE FUN!

If you make a mistake, don't get discouraged. The more you craft, the better you'll get it at. Make your crafting space a happy place. You've got this!

MY CRAFTING SPACE

My crafting space is the smallest room in my house, which shows that you don't need that much space! It's basically just a small table, a chair, and a desk. That's it.

There's a lot of storage, but I'm not very organized with my crafts. When you walk in there, there's stuff everywhere, glue everywhere, posters on the floor, and pom-poms all around. With makeup, I am more organized!

Even though my craft room is messy, it is my work space. So every time I walk in there, I know I have to get to work.

The crazy thing is like 90% of my videos are of me doing the craft on camera for the very first time. I'll see the craft in my head and I'll draw it. That way, I kind of know what I'm getting into. But it's almost always the very first time I'm making it!

My filming space is basically just my worktable. I'll add a colorful background and then turn on the three box lights that I use.

When we're filming, things get messy on set. Surprise!

FIDGET SPINNER TEMPLATE

You'll need an adult to help you.

1 Cut out this stencil, then lay it on top of foam board.

2 Use a pencil to carefully trace around it.

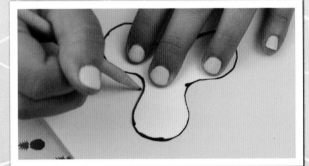

3 **ASK AN ADULT FOR HELP HERE.**

Make sure the foam board is lying on a flat surface. Cut out the shape with a hobby knife. That's it!

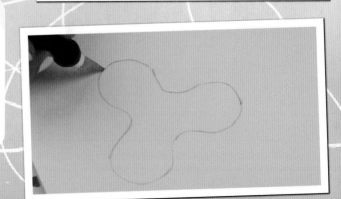

I want to say THANK YOU so much to all of my followers. You inspire me every single day and I wouldn't be who I am without you guys. You honestly mean the world to me. I hope you love this book. It's all because of you!

Say "hey" and show me your projects!

YouTube: /TheKarinaBear
Instagram: @Karingarc1a
Twitter: @Karinaa_Bear

BEFORE YOU GO . . .
MAKE SURE TO CHECK OUT MY FIRST BOOK!